# A Student of Melancholy

Poetry and Prose
by Marlene D. Pennington

**From the Author**

The first time I shared a poem with my father at the age of 30, I commented on how melancholic it was. He responded by saying, "you're a student of Poe."

And it's true. Edgar Allan Poe has been the author that I turn to time and again when my reality feels fuzzy and my feet feel unsteady. There is something in the bleakness of his writing that calms me, something familiar in the gray tones of his language. It feels like home.

I've never considered myself a poet. Poetry is something I have historically only written when I can't form coherent thoughts, when my world turns upside down. It took a cosmic coincidence for me to meet someone who would ultimately encourage and inspire me to share my words with people; someone to show me that perhaps my ability to convene with the darker shadows in my mind wasn't such a bad thing.

I have never titled a poem, the exception to this being the last poem in this collection. It is the first and only poem I have ever written that came to mind complete with title. I choose to date them instead, but I omit the year they were written. This is my first collection of poetry and prose. I hope to not inspire, but rather to comfort. I hope you find comfort in the shadows, as I have.

**Dedication**

The list of people to thank and dedicate this collection to is too long. I am touched in some way by every person I have ever met. But if I must name a few....

To every strong woman in my family who has encouraged me to find my own path, regardless of overgrown it may be.

To Shawn, for believing in me, and being the strongest, most constant friend I have ever had. One of the few in my life who remind me that my dreams are always just within reach.

To Joshua, for showing me that my type of creativity is just as beautiful as the type that inspires. I struggled for a decade to finish any 1 of the 3 novels I was working on, and with your quiet encouragement, I finished this in mere months. For helping me unbury a person I had thought gone forever. For helping me find my voice again.

To every person who plays in the shadows and befriends the monsters under their beds.

July 12

All alone as the moon crosses the sky.
All alone as the stars burn out and die.
No one to care or comfort me.
No one to care or even see
The terrible pain I hold inside.
All alone as the sun sits on the horizon
Casting its fiery glow over the world.

Hiding inside my shell
A haven I've come to cherish
No one seeks me.
Does anyone even notice
That I've gone away?
Still I say good bye.
Good bye to no one.

August 2

Sometimes I wish I could
Get lost in the world
If only to learn
That someone cared enough
To find me.

August 2

I wasn't supposed to fall in love with him. His eyes weren't supposed to remind me of the sweetest chocolate I have ever tasted. His touch wasn't supposed to make my knees weak. His kiss wasn't supposed to resonate through my soul. He wasn't supposed to be my first and last thoughts, every day. My name on his lips wasn't supposed to sound like a symphony. But there he is. Every day. Every day, I want him more than the last, despite my best efforts.

I feel my heartache in the distance, closing in. But in his eyes, I see everything I want. So I continue toward the pain, bracing myself for the fall, even as I let myself discover new things about him that make my heart sing. Is this madness? It must be. What other explanation is there? To go purposefully in the direction of ruin, smiling with each deliberate step? What sane person clearly sees their demise on the horizon and still moves towards it?

But perhaps love itself is madness. We love people despite every instinct to the contrary. We give one person the power to destroy us and hope they will not. We forgive those we love, regardless of how many times they have hurt us. We fall for people without reason. We see something in those that we love that no one else can see, and they call to us in a voice that only our souls can hear. Love does not follow a pattern, love does not listen to reason. Love is madness, chaos. But it is beautiful, breathtaking, in its chaos.

The problem with love is that it often blinds us to some of the most destructive aspects of the objects of our love. Or worse, we see quite clearly. But explain away anything negative, or justify our beloved's actions. We tolerate more from the people we love than from anyone else in our lives. We let them get away with more and tolerate behavior we condemn in others. It can be poisonous, deadly. We can lose ourselves, and become strangers to those around us.

But when love is good and healthy, oh how beautiful it can be.  Two fragile souls become one unstoppable force when love is strong, and respect is stronger.  Two people can conquer the world when they are in love.

## August 20

I open my eyes
And watch the light fade away
I lift my head
And watch the shadows roll in
The last of my tears
Drying on my cheeks
As darkness settles in

These familiar sensations
The pangs of loneliness
As silence falls around me
The welcome emptiness
While the world falls away

Why do I think I belong there
Why do I chase the light
It only burns me
When I get too close
Why do I fight the pull of the shadows
The sweet numbness and nothing
I know so well

I belong here
Where no one can find me
Where no one can hurt me
Where my heart is my own
I belong here
Where the shadows know my name
And the darkness holds me close.

August 20

Sometimes you find yourself in the shadows, drifting farther from the light, wondering how to get out. Wandering from one puddle of darkness to the next, hoping one may be lighter than the next. Sometimes the darkness consumes you, choking out even the brightest of lights. As the blackness thickens around you, and you close your eyes, feeling your heart race and your breath quicken, you allow yourself to let go of whatever foolish hope you may cling to. Hope cannot live in the darkness; it is suffocated by the shadows.

In the shadows, curled upon yourself, you face your doubts, your fears, your inadequacies. The darkness whispers of your failures, softly reminding you why you cower here. Maybe you find comfort in the shadows, because they are familiar. They greet you like an old friend, pulling you tightly into a lasting embrace.

Some of us are born for the shadows, born for those darker

places, the place that few venture. Some of us are able to navigate the shadows like a well-known path, one we travel all too often. That familiar pang of loneliness, the almost welcome sense of emptiness. We are so accustomed to these sensations, they barely register, and certainly do not frighten.

August 22

Would you run away with me
And hide from the world?
Would you leave this routine behind
And find adventure with me?
Would you open your heart
And let me love you?
If I promised to love all of you,
Even the darkest parts that you lock away
The darkness you loathe?

Would you take my hand
And walk into the night?
Eyes cast to the heavens,
Counting the stars?

September 7

She was the girl who told everyone that she couldn't sneeze when they notice the tears in her eyes. The girl who smiles every time someone cancelled plans with her, because she had other stuff to do anyway. The girl who held her friends close when they cried and gave them the comfort she craved.

She was the girl who spent her days cheering on all she knew, while she sat alone on the sidelines. She was the friend who faded into the background of every gathering. The one forgotten and left out of every get-together. The girl who was an expert at disappearing, because unless she really tried, no one noticed her anyway.

All of this she did with a smile, even as silent tears escaped her eyes and snuck down her cheeks.

She was one of the forgotten. One of the lonely ones. One of the people you wondered about years later when you realize you haven't heard from them in you-can't-remember how long.

She was the girl who eventually stopped trying and embraced the isolating darkness.  The girl who gave small pieces of herself to everyone she met, until there was nothing left.  The girl the world forgot.

October 22

Her eyes have lost that shine
That hopeful glimmer of youth.
Hurt too many times
Broken just a little much.
A dull expectation replaces the light
Waiting for the next disappointment.
She sees it
Lurking around the corner.
It doesn't sneak up on her anymore.
She waits patiently for it now.
Knowing that
While it may take its time
It will come just the same.

October 22

She fights the tears
Refusing to give in to the
breakdown.
No stranger to this battle
But weary all the same.
Tired in her heart
Tired in her soul
And still she fights.
Each wave of sorrow
Stronger than the last.
What she wouldn't give
For something
Anything
To make it go away.

She closes her eyes
Face turned to the heavens
And begs for strength.
Begs for peace.
But finally gives in.
Just for a moment.
She lets the tears fall.
Silent.
Like her pain.

November 8

I don't know how long I have you.
If it's just for tonight,
Or if I will get to see the passage of time on your face.
If it's only for a moment,
Or if I will get to notice each new wrinkle crease your skin.

I don't know how long I have you.
If your smile will be a brief glimpse,
Or if I will hold your hand as you pass into the next life.
If we will share only this night,
Or if we will make a lifetime of memories.

I don't know how long I have you.
But I know that I am thankful for every second.
I will love you,
Passionately and without question
Every moment I have you.
I will love you like I will lose you.

I don't know how long I have you.
But I will love you like you are my last.

December 2

Show me a fairytale
And I'll show you a vault of well kept secrets.
Show me two people in love
And I'll show you how they cover their fears.
Show me the perfect family
And I'll show you where they hide their arguments.
Show me an unbreakable woman
And I'll show you every tear stained volume she turns to for comfort.

Balance
Black and white
Good and evil
Love and hate
Two sides to every coin.

We only see one side
The side facing the world.
The stories face away,
Held tight to those that own them.

Show me someone who has everything
And I'll show you an empty soul.
Show me someone who always smiles
And I'll show you their misery.

You see what we let you see
The light side,
Because if you saw both sides,
You would never come back.
Your light is my darkness.

December 2

I like to be depressed sometimes. Some of my best creative moments happen when I am low; so low, it feels like the weight above may crush me. But it is a dangerous place to be. It is consuming. Easy to get lost in. Trying to find my way back out often leaves me tired, mentally and emotionally exhausted. Once I give myself to the darkness, it is almost like I forget what the light looks like; I forget what to look for to find my way out.

Some days, I don't mind being lost for a while. There is a sense of comfort in hiding in the shadows. No one sees me, and I suddenly stop caring about what is happening outside my small, intimate corner of the world. A rare moment of apathy often finds me. I feel as though the world could crumble around me and I would not care. It suddenly does not bother me that I could disappear for days and my absence would go largely unnoticed. These small apathetic moments worry me from time to time; they are jarring moments of clarity when I see exactly how inconsequential my existence is to the world around me. If I were no longer here, the world would continue to spin, people's lives would continue without me with little interruption.

I would normally expect these things to bother me, but when I find myself in these moods, I just cannot seem to garner the energy to care. I would rather just sleep the day away, lost in my dreams, or no dreams, which is often preferable.

I wonder from time to time, where these feelings, where this darkness, comes from. I frequently feel guilty about feeling hopeless sometimes. What reason do I have to be hopeless? I have a wonderful family, amazing parents, and want for nothing. And yet, there are days, nights, when I struggle to keep myself together, as though my carefully built personal empire may fall at any moment, and I am to blame. What is it about my oh-so-perfect existence that irks me? How can I feel anything less than blessed for all that life and its beautiful coincidences have given me?

I feel guilty about letting myself indulge in these selfish bouts of introspection and self-loathing. Instead of sleeping the day away, I could be writing, reading, helping the homeless, curing world hunger. Instead, I would rather lose myself in imaginary dream worlds, unconscious to the reality around me.

Is it just another way to hide? Why do I hide so much? Is it in the hope that someone, anyone, will find me? Despite my best efforts, have I become nothing more than yet another damsel in distress, begging for someone to save me? My moody spells acting as silent pleas for someone to be rescued?

Perhaps it is that ever present desire to be wanted, for your absence to matter to someone. Regardless of how adamantly we may disagree, or how stoic we appear, we all want to matter to someone. We all want our absence felt by someone; we want to feel like we fill a space in someone's life that no one else can, be it romantically or otherwise.

Perhaps that is why these dark places scare me... Because I know that no one notices me when I'm gone. They may note it as unusual, but write it off seconds later. My presence in so many people's lives is routine, expected, I wonder how many would notice I was missing? Or would they simply find it odd, a departure for the norm, and move on with their lives? How many would be genuinely concerned? How many would look for me? Who would seek me?

December 2

Sometimes I seek out the darkness,
Hoping it will open its arms to me,
One last time.
Pull me in,
Love me,
Like the rest of the world cannot.

Sometimes I chase the shadows,
Hoping they will let me in,
Let me play,
Because the world will not.

Sometimes I hide behind my smile,
Hoping no one can see,
The tears falling behind my eyes.

Sometimes I let my madness out to play,
Hoping to find someone just as mad,
Who wants to play too.

But every time,
Every day,
I am lost.
Wandering the empty streets of my mind,
Crying out for purpose,
Begging for meaning.
And I am met with only hollow echoes
Of a lost voice,
A beaten spirit,

Desperate for redemption.

December 4

As the seasons change
And the weather turns cold
Memories fly through my mind
It will be Christmas soon
But this year will be different
Not the same
I am alone for the holidays
Celebrating with only a photograph

The leaves are falling
The grass is freezing
The winds gusting
Carrying your voice
As the snow falls
As does my heart
Christmases come and go
They have all felt the same
But not this year
This year is different
This year is empty

December 15

On her knees
Hands over her ears
She screams into the night
Cries unheard
Pain ignored
She is just a shadow
Lost in the pavement

December 19

Do you remember who you were,
Can you picture the little girl of yesterday,
Before the world pressed down upon your shoulders,
Before you learned of hurt?

Can you see the dreams of your youth,
Do you remember the passion that made them burn,
Before each disappointment hardened your heart?

Can you hear the way you used to laugh,
Carefree and joyous,
Before you were taught to quiet your voice?

Does it hurt you now
To see how far you've fallen?
To remember a time you cannot return to,
To see a woman too far gone to find again?
Do you remember who you were?

December 19

Please let me hide
Let me disappear from this reality
Filled with hate and pain
Surrounded by death and tears

Please take me away
Far away from the scathing eyes
and poisonous voices

Please show me a safe place
A place I can be myself without fear
of contempt

Please bring back the love
The love that bound us together

Please give back the hope
The hope that we can make it better

Please take away the despair
Blanketing our world

If you can't do this
Then please just let me hide
Please let your gaze skirt my
cowering form
Desperately trying to disappear

December 20

If I disappeared
Would you wonder where I had gone?
If I stopped calling
Would you notice the silence?
If I slowly began to fade
Would you chase me
Squinting to keep me in focus?

Or would I just become a memory?
A person you used to smile with on occasion?
Would you let our memories fade,
Like an old polaroid,
Exposed too long,
Shadows and hints
Of what once was?

December 20

I hope someone
Some day
Find my books
My thoughts captured forever
On the pages
Between the covers
And thinks
*Oh, how I would have loved her…..*

December 20

I will always be that person
Who loves someone more

I will always be that person
Who sacrifices everything for
someone

I will always be that person
Who gracefully lets go
Watching them walk away
With my head held high

I will always be that person
Who says it's ok, I'm ok
While I'm breaking apart inside

I will always be that person
Who gives my all to someone
Taking nothing in return

I will always be that person
Who knows the bitter taste of
disappointment
Just a little too well.

December 21

Sometimes my words get stuck,
Lodged in my throat,
Trying to suffocate me.
When you're not around,
It's easy for me to think
Of everything I want to say.
But as soon as I see your face,
Hear your voice,
Feel your touch,
I lose everything,
Except the space between us.

Caught between telling you
everything
And not wanting to ruin the moment.
An endless tug of war,
With my brain and my heart.

In the end,
I stay silent,
Leaving the unspoken thoughts
For sleepless nights.

Because these small moments
together
Are everything I want.
And I am desperate not to spoil
them.
Because I know that when you are
gone,

These small moments,
Are the only things I will keep.

January 3

My first words of the New Year. I feel an unusual weight to them, as if they set the tone for the coming months. Will they be hopeful? Grateful? Loving? Melancholy? I feel as those these words carry the possibilities of the year in them. What will I fill them with?

I will fill them with resolve. The resolve to take each day as it comes. The resolve to give it my best shot from sun up until sundown. The resolve to understand that not every day will be great, and the resolve to try again when they are not. But beyond it all, I fill these words and the following days with the resolve to fight. To fight through the darkness. To fight through the bad days. To fight through it all.

January 4

She liked to walk at night
When the world was quiet and still.
She felt peaceful,
Privileged
To see this side of the world.

Undisturbed
Unconcerned with the troubles of the daylight.
She felt like part of a secret,
A secret the darkness kept just for her.
She felt like the stars twinkled just so
For her eyes only.
Like the air was sweeter
For her lungs alone.

The night was the most perfect partner,
Welcoming without question.
Listening without interruption.
Embracing without condition.

Sometimes it whispered,
So softly
For her to stay.
Stay in the darkness,
Where the world was hers.
She could have everything,
Anything she could ever want.

It was tempting,
The delicious promise of oblivion.
But she always resisted,
Fearing the loss of the daylight,
And everything she knew.

But tonight,
Tonight she ran.
She ran towards the endless void.
Plunging herself into the night,
Giving in to the darkness,
And its comforting arms.
The promise of quiet
And an end to the pain.
Tonight she gave into the shadows
And their whispered sweet nothings.
Without a glance behind
Or a thought to what she left,
She welcomed the blackness,
Like a cherished lover,
Wrapping it around herself,
Until she faded from the world,
Consumed by the night
Devoured by the shadows.
She closed her eyes,
Tears drying on her cheeks,
As the darkness took her,
And she sighed.
One word slipping through her pale lips,
One thought on her last breath:
Home.

January 7

I hide from the light
The shadows suit me better.
No one sees the flaws
The imperfections
The pesky little demons
Whispering in my ears.

You shine light in the corners
Desperate to chase away the dark.
You cower in the blank spaces
Looking for the monsters
Trying to outrun them.
I blow out the candles
Eager for the light to fade.
Calling to the things you fear
Coaxing them out to play.
This is my world
The dark and the misunderstood.
The feared and the shunned.
Those that you turn your back on
Are the ones I open my arms to.
While you run and hide
From the creatures in the dark
I seek them
Kindred spirits in the shadows.

January 8

So what do you do
When you run out of words
And you have nothing left to say?

So what do you do
When you can't explain the pain
And the void inside engulfs
everything?

So what do you do
When you run out of tears
And there's nothing left to feel?

Do you run to the darkness to hide?
Or you do scream to heavens
And pray for salvation?
Do you abandon this world
And leave it all behind?
Or do you swallow it all
And press on?
Into the void
Into the pain
Into the gnawing emptiness
Searching for a glimmer of light?
Daring to dream
Daring to hope

January 10

Hope is a cruel drug
Pulling you ever forward
Searching for something
That may never be.
Despite everything
Every instinct to turn back
Hope forces you onward
Taking you around the next bend.
And the next
And still on.
Believing that this time
Yes, this is the moment
That everything will change.
But still you wait for that moment
Each taunt dragging you down
Until you are too far gone
To turn back.
You've lost your way.
It's too late.
Lost to hope.
Lost.

January 11

The silence stretches between us
Heavy with the things we won't say.
Our hopes and fears
Kept to ourselves
Quieted by the past
When we learned to keep secrets.

Who will break first
And open the flood gates?
Or will we stay quiet?
And choke on our words?

January 12

Are you scared?
Is your stomach twisting in knots?
Is your heart racing?
Your palms sweating?

Then you know you are about to lose
Something truly amazing.
You watch it walk away
Without a backward glance.
And no matter how fast
Or how far you run
You know that you will never catch it.

And so you stay behind
Stuck in place.
Watching it fade away
Quiet tears trailing down your cheeks.
Searching for your voice
To say goodbye.
But it's too late.
It's gone.
And you are alone.

Alone with your breaking heart.
Listening to the silence
Heavy with all you should have said.
But you were scared.

And your stomach was in knots.
And your heart was racing,
Your palms sweating
As you let everything you love
Walk away.

January 12

Sometimes my demons shout so loud
They drown out everything good.
I want to hide in a corner
Away from the world
And scream back at them.
Stop tormenting me!
Please just leave me be!

Every flaw
Every mistake
Every inadequacy
Brought to light
So obvious
So glaring

How could anyone want me?
How could anyone care for me?
I am broken.
So broken.
Never enough.
But somehow always too much.

The shouts turn to laughter.
Their cackles mocking my tears.
Look how fragile she is
They seem to say.
So easy to destroy.
Let's watch her crumble.

Hands over my ears
Screams ripping through my throat.
I hate when the demons win
And I am left cowering
Shuddering in the corner
My shouts echoing through the
night.

January 17

Today I let the shadows win
I am too broken to fight
Too tired to push forward

Today I choose to lay down
To rest my weary head
And give my heart a break

Today I give in to the demons
To their constant nagging
And allow them this small victory

Today I know I am beaten
I know I will not win this time
And I cast my eyes down
Accepting my failure

Because I am too tired
Too broken
Too lost

January 17

Sometimes my thoughts make me dizzy
Spinning so fast around my head
Rarely settling in one place
Unable to focus
Frustrated with the elusiveness of peace
Here for a moment
So fleeting
It may as well have been my imagination
Pesky little pixies
Dancing outside my grasp
Taunting me
Evading my desperate reach
Leading farther into the shadows
Farther from the light
A wild goose chase
That leaves me lost

January 21

I could fill oceans
With the tears I've cried
I could drown the world
With my sorrow
And snuff out the sun
With the darkness I hold inside.
I could fill a library with the volumes
Of words I have not said
Conversations I have swallowed.
I could claim every star in the sky
With the wishes and dreams
I have watched die.

But I hide behind a laugh
A perfectly practiced smile
So no one will know.
These secrets are mine.
This darkness is mine.
These tears are mine.
This world is mine.

January 21

I will bring the heavens to its knees
To find you again.
May the gods be with those
Who stand in my way.
With fire in my veins
And wrath in my heart
I will scour the earth for you.
But only if you want me to.

January 21

I loved him like my favorite song.
A cherished sanctuary I could turn to
When I had nowhere else to go
When my mind was a little too crowded.
He would settle my thoughts
Ease my tensions
Conquer my fear.

But like a favorite song
Our love had a time limit.
It filled a small piece in my life
Before it was gone.
Assigned to the archives of memories
A volume I return to
From time to time
When I'm feeling wistful and nostalgic.

But I put it back on the shelves
And return to now.
To the silence of my life.
Because somehow
Nothing else sounds as good
As my favorite song.

January 21

Sometimes my memories sneak up
on me
Making it hard to breathe.
The smile of a stranger
Tilted just so.
The first notes of a familiar song.

Sometimes I smile.
Others I fight back tears.
So bittersweet.
A reminder that I was happy.
That if only for a moment
Everything was perfect.

January 26

She wears her scars like trophies
Testaments to all she has endured.
Her tattered heart stitched together.
And back again.
Held in one piece
By pride and will alone.

Scraped knees from her many stumbles.
Bloody knuckles from every fight
To stay standing.
Tall and unapologetic
Fierce and headstrong.

But behind those determined eyes
Is a soul crying out for help.
Someone to stand by her side
And help carry the weight
Pressing down on her shoulders.
Someone who sees through the mask
To the broken child within.
Someone to say
I see you.
Let me hold your burden.
Rest your heart.
It is safe here.
You are safe here.

January 30

How many nights must I lie awake
Your name fading on my lips
Before I will finally dream?

How many tears must I cry
Hidden and alone
Before I will be able to smile?

How many lies must I endure
A smile painted on my face
Before I will hear the truth?

How many lines must I write
Each one a confession
Before you decide to read them?

I'm losing count
Of all the ways I have tried.
I'm losing faith
In everything I thought I knew.
I'm losing hope
That someday I may be enough.

January 30

I wish I knew how to write of happier things
Of sunshine and warmth
Of love and wonder.

I wish I knew how to write of hope
Of a summer's breeze and freedom
Of dreams and possibility.

Instead my words know only darkness
Demons and despair
Shadows and ruin.

My words bleed black
Poisoned by disappointment.

February 1

I lay my heart at your feet
And pray that you do not step on it.
I know it's not the prettiest
Or the most glamorous.
It might be a little frayed around the edges
Maybe a little worse for wear.
But I promise
It still works.

I don't blame you of course
If you don't want it.
After all
Why would you?
Who would want something so torn and tattered
Stitched together
Piece by broken piece.

I understand.
But please
If you don't mind
Be gentle
When you give it back.

February 14

You will ruin me
I feel it just as I feel
My heart racing in my chest

I see the heartache on the horizon
The impending tears
Like clouds in the distance
Rolling closer

Like the electricity in the air
Before the storm
I know that it's coming
But I don't know when.

All I can do is smile
As the light begins to fade
One moment closer

I brace for the inevitable
Happy just the same
For what little time
I was allowed
To bask in the sun

February 23

Some of us are born for broken
hearts
For rainy days and sad songs
Some of us are made for despair
For the color black and unanswered
prayers
We are the misfits
The misunderstood and outcast
We are students of melancholy
And masters of the shadows

February 27

It has taken me a long time to embrace the darker pieces of my personality. I have always thought I need to be happy, I need to be bubbly. I need to hide the parts of myself that people don't understand. So I have hidden my writing, ashamed to be so connected with the monsters in my head. It took meeting someone very special for me to understand that some of us are born with the ability to shine a light in those dark corners, to talk to the demons and hear what they have to say, without getting lost.

I've learned to love my style of creativity, and that it is necessary to my survival. I give a voice to the whispers in my mind so they don't drown out the world. They are acknowledged, and heard, and therefore kept at bay.

I've learned that giving voice to these creatures gives me balance. By acknowledging them, I understand them for what they are, and I willingly visit them from time to time. I happily walk into the shadows on occasion to connect with them, because then they don't seek me out as often, they allow me the space to enjoy the sunshine as well.

I have come to love my demons, rely on them even. I enjoy our conversations and the small pieces of wisdom they impart on me. I love them for the creativity they spark in me. They are always there, always accessible, always welcoming.

March 1

Twisted and knotted
A maze of confusion
Which way is out?
How do I go back?
Everything looks the same
I'll never find my way

Desperately searching
For something familiar
Something to guide me home
But everything is strange
So confusing
How can I find my way
When everything looks the same?

March 3

Someday I hope you see
The damage you've caused
And the scars you've left

Someday I hope you see
The destruction you've left
And the lives you've ruined

I hope it breaks your heart
And brings you to your knees
I hope it shatters your world
And destroys your soul
Like you destroyed mine

Someday I hope you look back
Regret heavy in your heart
And finally see
The trail of broken souls
You left in your wake.

March 3

Melancholy is my religion
And I worship
By the light of the moon
Hidden from the world
Where I belong
A place most hope to escape
It is here I make my home
Here I return to
Time and again
This is my safe haven
Because I know this

The gospels of the night
Are my guide
The sweetest lullaby
The silence in the air
Is a sanctuary
For my tormented mind
And my weary soul

March 3

She used to be strong
Her shoulders squared
Ready to take on the world
She used to be confident
So sure of herself
And her place in the world

She used to smile
Without reservation
Without hesitation
Her laugh could fill
The largest of rooms

Her weakness surprises her now
How quickly she retreats
Back into herself
Eyes trained to her feet
Praying she disappears

The only sounds echoing now
Are her choked sobs
The tears she fights
To keep from falling
And her whispered pleas
For salvation
For an answer
An end to the bleak reality
She has to come to know

March 9

I feel the distance setting in
See the distraction in your eyes
As you stare back at me
My pleas fall on deaf ears
My sadness met with apathy

It's only a matter of time
The clock ticking down
To our last good bye

But still I try
Desperately
To hold on

I feel you slipping away
My grip tightening
As yours loosens
A tear falls down my cheek
As you turn away

Lost and alone
I watch your shadow
Fade on the horizon

It didn't matter
How much I loved you
It didn't matter
How hard I tried
It didn't matter

You still walked away
Without a backward glance
You left me behind
A memory quickly forgotten
Like a scent in the air
Carried away on the breeze
A brief moment in time

I was a chapter in your book
But you were my story

March 10

Sometimes it's all too much
The weight of the world
The weight of expectation
The fear of disappointing everyone
Paralyzes me

Sometimes it's all too much
Facing the world with a smile
When all I want to do is cry
Hide away from everything
And wrap the shadows around me

Sometime it's all too much
Pretending to be ok
When inside I'm breaking apart
Fragile pieces of myself
Falling away

Sometime it's all too much
The effort to keep myself together
And be what everyone needs
While my soul is shaking
And my resolve weakening

Somehow I hold on
Even when I want nothing more
Than to let go


Is it the fear of failure

That keeps me holding on?
Is it the fear of disappointing
someone?
Or is something as foolish as hope?
The hope that I matter?
The hope that it will change?
The hope that maybe I'm wrong?
Despite it all
Do I hold on and believe
The beautiful lie
That is hope?

March 10

I can't do this again
She thinks to herself
Not again
I don't have the energy
I don't have the strength
But she doesn't know
How not to
How not to love
How not to care
How not to give a piece of herself
To every broken soul she meets
Because she knows
How it feels to be so empty
So lost
Completely hopeless

So she gives
She gives her love
Her trust
Her hope
Until she's given so much
That she simply fades away
A legacy of broken pieces
Given away
To put others back together
The only mark she leaves

March 14

If someone gave me a book
And that book
Was the story of our love
And they told me
How it would end
I would read it anyway
Every sentence
Every paragraph
Every page
And when I got to the end
Tears falling from my eyes
I would read it again

*When the Shadows Whisper*

I will destroy you
Quietly
Methodically
I will tear you down
One piece at a time
I will ruin you
And you can't stop it
I will break you
Completely
And smile through it all

www.ingramcontent.com/pod-product-compliance
Lightning Source LLC
Chambersburg PA
CBHW071414040426
42444CB00009B/2239